WHY DO I STINK?

Michelle Thornhill

For Alice

First Printing, 2019

ISBN 978-1-9992620-1-3

Readosaurus Press

There are plenty of nice smelling things in a flower garden.
This tiny little egg, which was laid in the soil of an otherwise fragrant
flower garden, was not one of them. It stunk!

You might think it was a rotten egg, but it wasn't. Something was growing inside. And if you could listen very closely you would hear a little voice asking "where am I?"
But for the longest time, no one answered.

The egg hatched. Out came a smelly little bug, no bigger than a strawberry seed. He looked at the huge world all around him.

"Who am I?" asked the smelly little bug.

The bug grew bigger and bigger. Each day he asked "what am I?"

One morning he got an answer.
"You are a majestic spider!" said a worm.
The bug was not a spider.
The worm didn't have much
of a brain, but he had a
big heart.

"I am?" said the little bug, very pleased.
"Spiders are very crafty. I will try to make a web."

The little bug heaved and puffed, trying to make spider silk, but all that came out was smelly bug poo.

"Ugh!" cried the bug. "This is very frustrating! Why can't I make a web?"

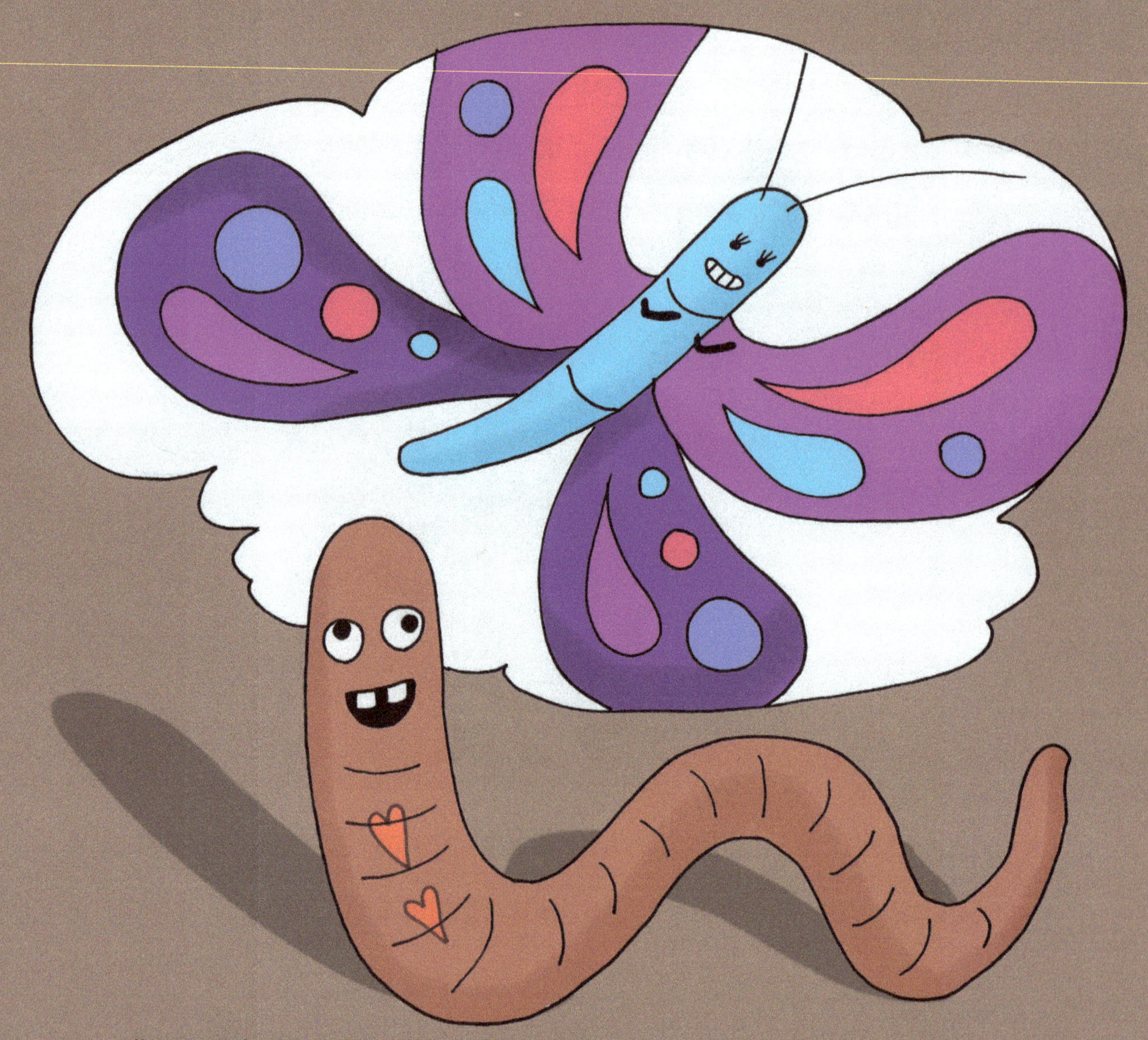

"Beautiful butterflies like you are supposed to fly away from webs," said the worm. He wasn't very good at thinking. But he had a big heart. In fact, he had two very big hearts.

"Wonderful!" said the smelly little bug. "I'm gonna fly!" He climbed up a daisy stem, took a running start, and immediately fell to the ground. He landed flat on his face. Splat!

"Owwwww!" cried the smelly little bug. "I failed! Why can't I fly?"
"Because you are a mighty, hardworking ant with no time to flutter
about!" The worm had a bad memory. But he had three very big hearts.

"Fantastic! Ants are very strong!" said the smelly little bug, jumping to his feet. "Let's see what I can do!" He tried to pick up a garden snail. "Errrrrrrrgh!" he grunted. "Gaaaaah! Oops!"

He took a step, but he stumbled and slipped. The snail flew out of his hands and he flopped to the ground.

The little bug was out of breath. "I can't lift anything! Why am I so weak?"

"Because you are a delicate damselfly!" said the worm. He was so confused, he had already forgotten that the smelly little bug couldn't fly. But he had four big hearts.

"Oh, thank you!" said the smelly little bug. "Damselflies shine like jewels! I will go sit on a flower where someone can admire me."

And that's what he did.

Before too long, a girl came along. "Look at this cool looking thing!" she said, looking at the flower. The little bug grinned. "How beautiful I must be!" he thought.

But when the girl bent
down to smell the flower
she shrieked,."Yuuuck!
That bug stinks!"
She plinked him off with
a long stick.

The little smelly bug was flung a short distance and landed in a pile of wet cow manure. He was not hurt, but he was sad and smellier than ever.

"It's not fair!" he cried, when the worm came to see if he was okay. "I can't make silk, I can't fly, I'm not strong, I'm not beautiful, and worst of all, I stink! WHY DO I STINK?"

The worm wasn't very smart. But now he smelled it, and even with his tiny brain he knew the answer. The little bug was a stink bug.

But the worm, like all earthworms, had five big hearts. So he didn't say anything.

The worm wrapped himself around the stink bug and gave him a hug. They sat in silence for a long time.

Eventually, the snail caught up to them. "Heyyyy," said the snail, slowly. "Don't..... try... to.... lift ...me!"

They were having such a good giggle about the snail being super slow that they didn't see the flock of birds landing nearby. "Did you hear something?" asked the smelly little bug.

But before anyone had time
to answer, a humongous beak
came down and snatched up
the worm and the bug
with it.
"Aaaaaaaargh!" yelled the
little brown bug, letting off a
puff of stink.

"Ewww, gross!" squawked the bird. "You are disgusting, dude." He dropped them both and flew away, taking the other birds with him.

At first, both the bug and the worm were too stunned
to say anything.
Finally the stink bug spoke. "That.... was..... AWESOME!"

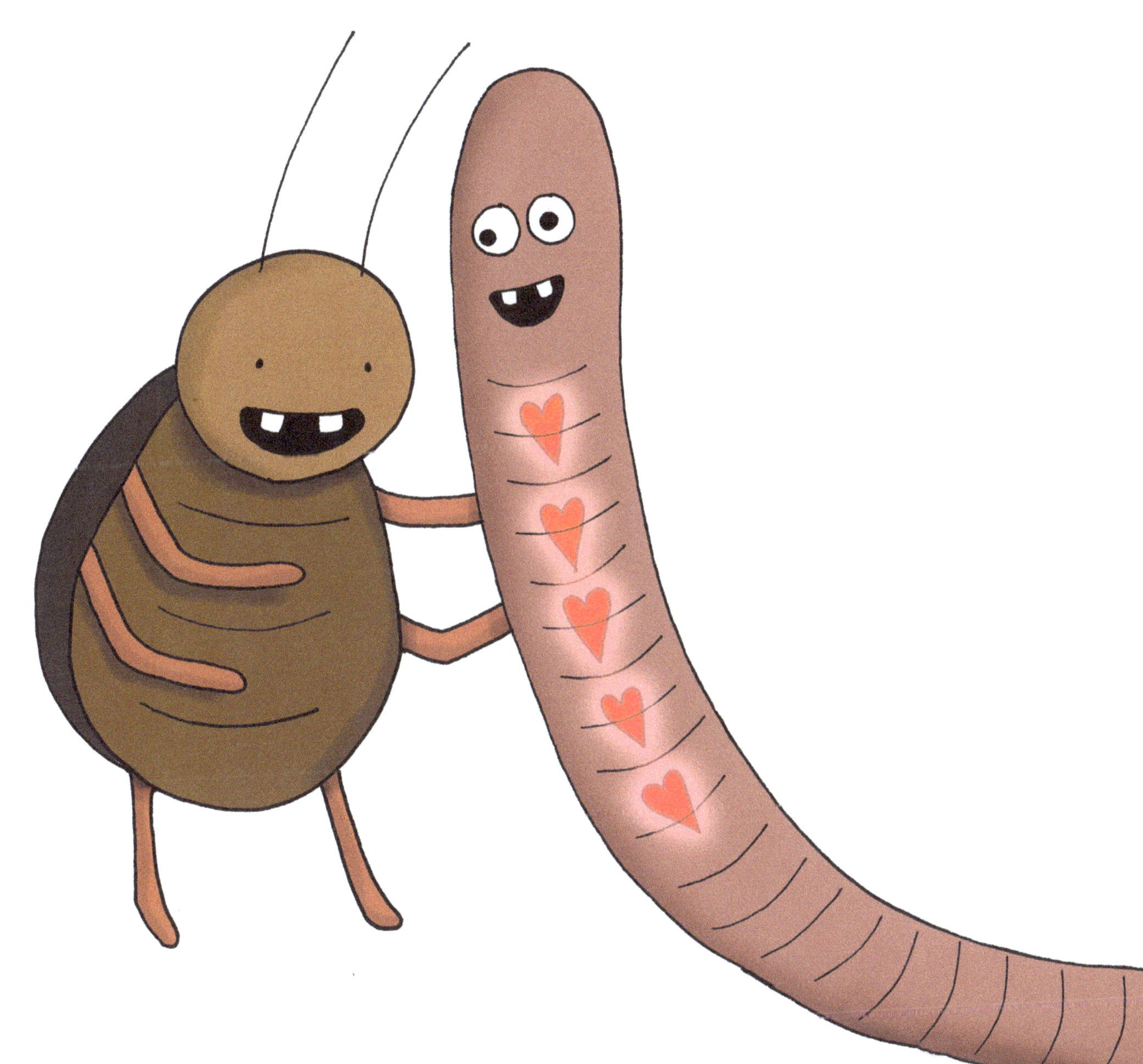

"That's because you are you, Stinkbug." said the worm.
His five hearts glowed.

A HUNDRED HOURS LATER

the snail said, "I... think... you...might...be...a...stink...bug."